'Don't believe that I can offer you an easy life. I hope you have no illusions about that.' With these words, the Shah of Iran warned Soraya Esfandiari that their marriage would not be simple. But he could not predict that one day he would have to make a decision that would shatter their happiness forever – that one day he would have to choose between his beautiful Princess and his beloved country.

Hulton Picture Company

MAKING OF A KING

FORCED INTO AN UNSUCCESSFUL ARRANGED MARRIAGE AT 19 AND THRUST INTO THE ROLE OF RULER WHEN THE WORLD WAS AT WAR, MOHAMMED REZA ENDURED A TURBULENT LIFE BEFORE HE MET SORAYA

Mohammed Reza, seen* above *at the age of eleven, was born into a military household in the walled city of Tehran

Reza Shah was in his forties when the children of his second marriage, to Tadj-ol-Molouk, were born. In spite of his eminence, he maintained a simple lifestyle. He usually wore his Cossack uniform* below, *and spent what time he could with his young children* left to right, *Mohammed, Shams and Ashraf

LITTLE COULD A BABY BOY, BORN ON 26 October 1919 to a humble family that lived in a modest house in the suburbs of Tehran, know that one day he would inherit such lofty titles as King of Kings, Light of the Aryans, Vice-Regent of God, Shadow of the Almighty and Centre of the Universe. But the boy had an eager father who secretly fostered heady ambitions, not just for his family but also for his country – Persia, as it was then called.

When Mohammed Reza, the boy who was to become king, was born, Persia was in turmoil. Britain was just one of many countries that viewed it as a cherry, ripe for the picking. While the greedy nations squabbled over who should control Persia, a country rich in oil reserves, an able soldier rose up through the ranks of the elite Persian Cossacks to become a general. Reza Khan, Mohammed's father, saw an opportunity for himself and he built up an army that was to oust the British.

On 26 October 1923, Reza Khan made himself Prime Minister and banished the reigning Shah Ahmad into exile in France. Having established himself as the most powerful man in the country, Reza Khan soon instructed Parliament to make him Shah, or king. As Mohammed was later to say, 'In Iran, as in America, it has always been possible for exceptional people to rise from the bottom to the top. My father provided an example of just that.'

The making of an heir

Reza Khan crowned himself in the mirrored throne room at the Golestan Palace in Tehran on 25 April 1926 and chose the title Reza Shah Pahlavi. Mohammed was simultaneously dubbed Valiahd, meaning Crown Prince. The sense of occasion was not lost on the youngster: 'You can imagine the awe it inspired in a six-year-old like me,' he reminisced later.

In his later years, Mohammed said, 'In my case my father influenced me more than anyone else.' Remarkable for his simplicity of taste and his personal conduct, Reza Khan was strong-minded, sober and hardworking. Although he could be tender and loving, even lighthearted, with his family, he had firm ideas on what his son should be and how he should behave. He made him an army colonel when he was seven and told him, 'Give the impression you are in control of everything. Trust nobody.' It was a simple philosophy which

Harlingue-Viollet

CREATOR OF A DYNASTY

Reza Khan, Mohammed's father *right*, was a commoner, one of 32 children born to the seven wives of Colonel Abbas Ali Khan, an officer of the regular Persian army. On assuming the Peacock Throne, Khan became an absolute and ruthless ruler who slaughtered many thousands of his people in order to secure his position. He was both feared and respected by his subjects.

One of his first decrees on coming to power was that every Iranian should take a family name as, up until then, most Iranians went by their given names alone. For himself he picked 'Pahlavi', an ancient word for the Persian language. He reckoned that this would link him and his dynasty with the glories of Ancient Persia.

Among his other edicts were that Persia should be called Iran, which means 'Aryan' in the native language, and that women should not be obliged to wear the *chodor*, or veil. However admirable this last advice is in Western eyes, it is still contrary to strict Islamic (Shi'ite) law.

His practical achievements included the start of construction work on the trans-Iranian railway, numerous roads and several shipping ports. 'Reza Shah started the transformation of Iran – and starting is very important,' an Iranian oil executive remarked in the 1980s

Camera Press

After his father became Shah, Mohammed **below left, in the white belt** ***received an elementary education at a small military school for the sons of army officers and government officials. His 20 classmates were specially selected by the Shah's advisors***

The Le Rosey Institute, a Swiss boarding school, was much more to the taste of the young Valiahd He became a keen sportsman, and in 1935 he captained the school soccer team **below** ***through a successful season. The following year, he returned to military school in Iran***

Popperfoto

♔ ***Mohammed returned in 1936 to an Iran that was fast being Westernized. He studied for two years at the military college in Tehran, which was modelled on the French academy at St Cyr. While there, he was often visited by his father* left, *who gave him political instruction***

♔ ***Reza Shah chose Princess Fawzia of Egypt* right *to be his son's wife. Not only was she suitably high-born, but she would serve to bring Egypt and Iran closer together. The only possible objection to her was that the Constitution required both parents of any future ruler to be of Persian blood. Reza Shah instructed his parliament to push through a law rescinding this provision***

♔ ***The Crown Prince* below *graduated in 1938 as a second lieutenant. He began work as an inspector in the army, while enjoying a lively social life in which fast cars and nightclubs featured strongly. Unknown to him, his father was manoeuvring to find him a wife***

Mohammed was to put to good use some 50 years later.

Although the newly-crowned Shah had great aspirations for Mohammed, he occasionally doubted that his heir had the necessary spirit to become a supreme ruler. For a start, he was a sickly child and nearly died from successive bouts of malaria, diphtheria and typhoid. Moreover, most of the Crown Prince's childhood had been sprnt in the company of women. While the King was away, ruthlessly subjugating the nomadic sheiks opposed to his rule, Mohammed remained at home, the darling of the royal household which was dominated by his headstrong mother, Tadj-ol-Molouk. He was also extremely close to his twin sister, Princess Ashraf.

> ***'In my case my father influenced me more than anyone else'***
>
> MOHAMMED REZA

An unhappy childhood

To counter what he perceived to be weakening influences, Reza Khan directed that his son receive 'a manly education'. Isolated from his mother, his sisters, his Meccano set, and his treasured bicycle, he was banished to live in a separate household within the palace grounds, presided over by a French governess whose principal task was to familiarize him with Western culture. Clad in an uncomfortable army uniform, Mohammed spent his daylight hours at a military elementary school that had been specially created for him and the sons of government ministers. When he was just eight, the child was obliged to take military salutes and had to endure lengthy meetings of the Shah's high council.

When the Shah was in town, which was not often, Mohammed's days were punctuated with ritual luncheons with his father – not the pleasurable experiences they might have been. Recalling his unhappy childhood to Soraya many years later, he said, 'We were all frightened of him. He needed only to fix his piercing eyes upon us and we went rigid with fear and respect.'

Swiss schools

When Mohammed turned 13, the Shah decided that his son's European education should be extended, and so he was sent to Switzerland, where he attended two schools. At first he attended a day-school, the Ecole Nouvelle de Chailly, and then he progressed as a boarder to Le Rosey Institute, an elite establishment that nestled on the shores of Lake Geneva.

There is a story that when the heir to the Peacock Throne stepped out of his luxurious, canary-yellow, Hispano-Suiza car on arriving for his first day at Le Rosey, he demanded that all the other students should stand to attention. An insulted American boy, according to the tale, promptly stepped forward and felled the upstart Valiahd with a single blow, whereupon the future Shah straightened himself up and shook the American by the hand.

At Le Rosey the prince developed into a physically strong young man. Perhaps surprisingly, he became a popular pupil, too, excelling at sport and ultimately captaining the school soccer team. He delighted in the democratic lifestyle encouraged by the staff but ultimately hc paid the penalty for fraternizing with people below his status. A zealous guardian soon heard of his activities and thereafter, while his friends were allowed to socialize at local parties, Mohammed was confined to quarters under the watchful eye of a bodyguard.

During these idle hours, when, no doubt, he envied his schoolmates' freedom, the

Hulton Picture Collection

Popperfoto

lonely Valiahd struck up a friendship with a man ten years his senior. Ernest Perron was the son of the school gardener and regarded himself as a talented poet. Mohammed remained firm friends with Perron throughout his life and latterly heaped favours on him, much to Soraya's chagrin.

Military training

Fearing poetry to be a weakening influence – and conveniently forgetting the legacy of Omar Khayyam – the Shah withdrew his son from Switzerland, and in the spring of 1936 sent him to Iran's Military College.

Mohammed had little respite during his two years at military school. In between the commando training and night exercises, his father took him on excursions around Iran to familiarize him with the nation he was destined to rule. They travelled in an ancient Rolls Royce which was ill-equipped to tackle the dirt roads. When the car broke down, as it frequently did, the Shah and his son would seek refuge in the nearest village. First, however, the King of Kings would order all the local dogs killed – he could not tolerate howls in the night.

Pursuit of a suitable partner

After his stint at military college, during which time he learned to speak and write English, Mohammed graduated as a second lieutenant and took up a position as an inspector in the army. Discovering a new independence and overcoming his innate shyness, the Crown Prince became something of a playboy. He bought a string of sports cars and frequented night clubs. 'I was a popular Crown Prince,' Mohammed recalled wistfully as he approached the end of his life.

Revelling in the fast life was not some-

AN EXTENDED FAMILY

Reza Khan indulged in the Islamic privilege of having several wives, four in all, and consequently Mohammed had an extended family which included a bewildering array of step-mothers and half-siblings.

Mohammed's all-powerful, real mother – Tadj-ol-Molouk (Crown of the King) *right, centre* – had four children: *left to right* Princess Shams, Mohammed (the Shah), Prince Ali and Princess Ashraf. Also under the care of Tadj-ol-Molouk was Reza Khan's first child, a daughter whose mother died in labour.

Reza Khan's other two wives, who lived in individual households, give birth to four more sons: the princes Gholam, Abdul, Ahmad and Mahmoud

Camera Press

Topham

♔ *Mohammed and Fawzia were married in March 1939* above. *The bride was given in marriage by her brother, King Farouk. Fawzia* right, *was considered a great beauty. Mohammed was said to have fallen in love with her photograph, but to have been doubly smitten when they met for the first time on Farouk's yacht*

Popperfoto

thing of which the ascetic Shah approved, and, unbeknown to his son, he dispatched envoys around the Islamic world to seek out a woman who would make him a suitable bride. His instructions were simple: the girl had to be a high-ranking Muslim, submissive, beautiful and, above all, a virgin.

Princess Fawzia of Egypt, daughter of the late King Faud and sister of King Farouk, fitted the Shah's ideal perfectly, and he proposed to the Egyptian leader that the two young people should marry. Farouk, seeing the possibilities of getting his hands on Iranian oil, agreed the deal and the monarchs duly exchanged photographs of the prospective couple.

'The first thing I knew, I was betrothed,' said Mohammed later. 'Up to that point I had never set eyes on the girl.'

Two weddings

The 19-year-old Crown Prince married his first Princess twice. The first marriage was a formal signing of papers in Cairo, the second was a religious affair on 15 March 1939 in Tehran. Reza Khan, ever one to boast of his power, welcomed the Princess to the Iranian capital and, as he patronisingly waved to the crowd, intoned, 'My child, your country and your people.'

The Shah was glibly smug once the contracts had been sealed. Like Mohammed, the Princess had been educated in Switzerland and, on the face of it, the couple had much in common. 'After all,' the Shah probably mused, 'They both enjoy horse riding, dancing and watching Hollywood films.' After the wedding celebrations, the young couple lived for a time in the Marble Palace, a beautiful building of translucent greenish stone which the Shah had constructed. These early months of marriage were happy and carefree.

> ***'The first thing I knew, I was betrothed . . . I had never set eyes on the girl'***
>
> MOHAMMED REZA

The news for which the Shah had been waiting was announced early in 1940. The Princess was pregnant. The aging despotic ruler could hardly disguise his excitement . . . nor his anguish when the baby was a girl. 'It is a bad sign when a girl is born in a court before a boy,' he fumed. The child, Princess Shahnaz, did not get a unanimously warm welcome into the world, although for her parents, her birth marked, as Mohammed later observed, the 'happiest point' in their marriage.

The new Shah

However, the war years had come and in 1941, when British and Russian troops invaded Iran, the Shah abdicated.

'I found myself plunged into a sea of

Popperfoto

♔ ***In the year or so after their wedding, the young couple spent a great deal of time together*** right, ***travelling all over Iran. They hunted, swam and played tennis together, leading a carefree, irresponsible life***

Topham

♔ ***Fawzia gave birth to a girl, Shahnaz, in 1940 but though the young family posed happily together in the royal palace*** below ***in 1942, the new Shah's marriage had already begun to founder, particularly when there was no sign of a male heir***

trouble,' recalled Mohammed. Not only was he virtually powerless while his country was occupied, but his personal life was in disarray as well. His father, who had promised him eternal advice and support, went to South Africa to live in exile and the novice king received little help at home.

The marriage breaks down

For some time, rumours had been circulating in Tehran that Mohammed and his wife were far from content. The tittle-tattle was largely true, although stories of his cruelty to the Princess were roundly repudiated. Princess Fawzia, who had grown up in the sumptuous luxury of the Egyptian royal court, found Tehran drab. She found the new Shah drab. She found anything and everything to do with Iran drab. In essence, she was homesick; she was the spoiled child of a privileged background that dated back centuries. The final straw that motivated her decision to move into private quarters, within the grounds of the Golestan Palace, was enmity between her and her mother-in-law, Tadj-ol-Molouk.

After peace had been declared in Europe, the Shah succeeded in ending the British and Russian occupation of Iran. His diplomatic skills won him international renown and many of his people supported him as well. However, the Princess Fawzia was not among his admirers, and in 1947 she elected to return to her native land, taking Princess Shahnaz with her.

By the time their divorce was granted on 19 November 1948, there was little love lost between the Shah and his first wife. Indeed, he was happy to be a free man once again.

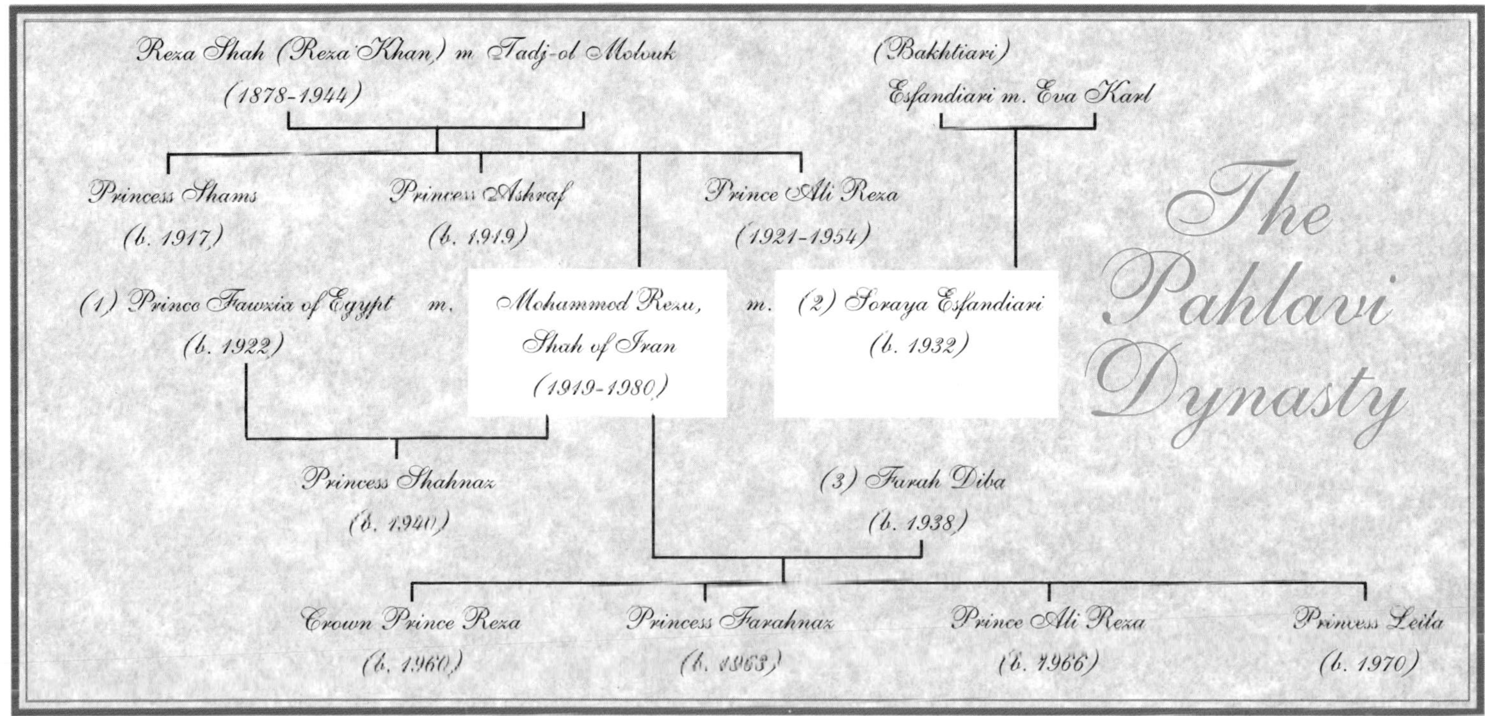

Family Album

Popperfoto

Hulton Picture Company

Camera Press

♔ *Princess Ashraf, the Shah's twin sister* above, *described as 'courageous and intelligent' by her admirers and as 'ambitious and scheming' by her detractors. The Shah appointed her Iran's representative at the United Nations and in the 1970s she was Chairman of the UN Commission on Human Rights. With her mother, she was one of the first women in Iran to refuse to wear the veil*

♔ *Princess Fatima, the Shah's half-sister, with her first husband, Vincent Lee Hillyer, an American student* above. *The marriage incurred the Shah's disapproval until Hillyer converted to the Muslim religion. Fatima's second husband was General Khatami, the loyal pilot who flew the Shah and Queen Soraya into exile in 1953. He was killed in a hang-gliding accident in 1975*

♔ *Prince Ahmad Reza* left, *the Shah's third half-brother. He was one of the four sons born to Reza Shah's favourite and fourth wife, Esmat (Chastity)*

The Shah's Brothers and Sisters

Camera Press

♔ ***This family photograph*** **above** ***was taken in 1950 on the occasion of the marriage of Prince Abdul Reza, the Shah's second half-brother and a graduate of Harvard university, to Princess Simin, the daughter of the president of Iran's Melli Bank. The group consists of*** **left to right** ***Prince Abdul Reza and Princess Simin; Princess Fatima; Prince Ali Reza (killed in a plane crash in 1954); and the Shah's eldest sister, Princess Shams (seated)***

Camera Press

♔ ***A photograph of the youthful Princess Ashraf with one of her husbands. She married three times, first to a socialite picked by her father. Her second husband was an Egyptian, Ahmad Shafiq, who became Iran's Director of Civil Aviation but was sent into exile, with his wife, by Mossadeq. After another divorce, Ashraf married an attractive Iranian lawyer, Mehdi Bushehri, whom she met in Paris***

Camera Press

♔ ***Prince Mahmoud Reza, another of the Shah's half-brothers by his father's fourth wife. The brothers were prevented from succeeding to the throne because their mother was a Qajar and no one with the blood of the previous dynasty of Shahs was allowed to rule Iran by constitutional law***

RICHES UNIMAGINED

The fabled treasures of Persia are one of the most dazzling collections of jewellery and ornaments the world has ever seen. Their history stretches back to centuries before the birth of Islam or Christianity and includes the artistic masterpieces made for 19th century dynasties. Here are diamonds, pearls and rubies in vast profusion, some gifts from foreign kingdoms. During the Shah's reign fabulous Crown Jewels of Iran were on display in Tehran's Melli Bank

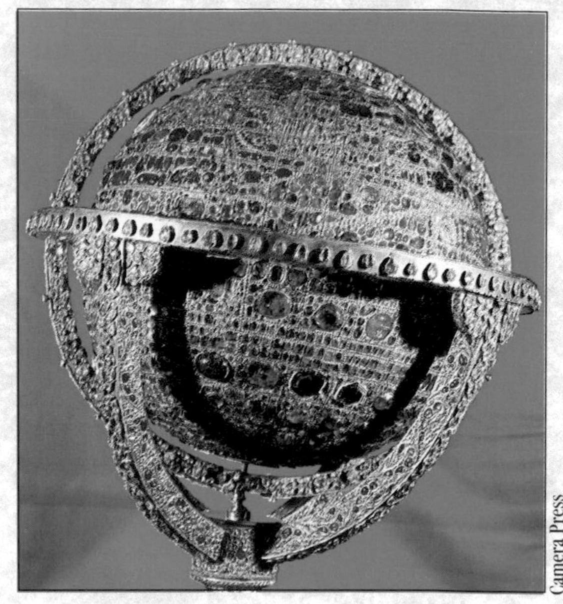

Camera Press

♔ *The Globe of Jewels* above *was completed in 1869, to the order of Nasr-ud-din-Shah. Over 51,000 jewels, weighing 18,200 carats, are encrusted in its frame and stand of fine gold. The world's seas are marked by emeralds and the land mainly by rubies. Britain, Iran and parts of Asia are set in diamonds. The globe is nearly two feet in diameter. Before it was constructed, the jewels were kept, unseen, in sealed leather bags*

William MacQuitty

♔ *The Daria-i-Nur diamond* above *is the centrepiece of the Iranian Crown Jewels. The name means Sea of Light. Measuring 1½ inches long, one inch wide and three eighths of an inch thick, it weighs 182 carats and is believed to date back to at least 558B.C.*

Camera Press

♔ *The sumptuous Kiani Crown* right, *thickly set in pearls, rubies and diamonds, was made in the reign of Fath Ali Shah's Qajar (1798–1834) as a Coronation Crown. The two Shahs of the Pahlavi dynasty chose not to be crowned with this Qajar symbol*

♔ *This golden narghile, or hookah,* above *set with turquoises and rubies, achieves a beautiful harmony of form and colour. It was made in Iran in the later 19th century and, like all the Crown Jewels, was not the personal property of the Shah but was used as collateral for the Iranian currency. The Royal Family had to sign receipts if they borrowed the jewels, and send them back to the Central Bank promptly*

♔ *The Iranian artistry in designing table vessels is illustrated by this gold and enamelled bottle* right *set with unusually large diamonds. The stopper is capped with a large ruby and ornamented with pearl drops. The bottle was made in the second half of the 19th century. Rarely used for practical purposes, it was designed for show, its array of jewels being a measure of royal luxury*

William MacQuitty

Popperfoto

REAL LOVE

RELEASED FROM THE BONDS OF HIS FAILED FIRST MARRIAGE, THE YOUNG SHAH INDULGED IN AFFAIRS WITH SOME OF THE MOST BEAUTIFUL WOMEN IN THE WORLD. THEN ONE DAY HE SAW A VISION OF PERFECTION. HER NAME WAS SORAYA

The fresh-faced Soraya Esfandiari* above, *destined to be the next Queen of Iran, was still at finishing school in Switzerland when the Shah divorced Fawzia

EXPLOITING HIS NEW-FOUND FREEDOM, as well as his increasing wealth and power as a ruler, the Shah embarked on a succession of carefree escapades in the two years following his divorce from Princess Fawzia. When he was not engrossed in affairs of state, the dashing King frequented dimly-lit nightclubs in Paris, Rome and London. More often than not, a good-looking girl clutched his arm. His reputation as a fast-living, fast-driving playboy and bon viveur became legendary.

Stars and strife

In his time, he had liaisons with international film stars such as Martine Carol, Yvonne de Carlo, Silvana Mangano and Gene Tierney. However, his affairs with these screen beauties were not long-lasting; he was essentially a lonely and troubled man. In her memoirs, his beloved Soraya wrote, 'As far as I know he never considered marrying any of these other women. He had far too much common sense for that.'

When he was not romancing, the Shah, still only in his late twenties, was obliged to wrestle with the political strife that threatened the stability of his country. By the end of World War Two, Iran had become the fourth largest producer of oil in the world. Many countries were envious of the country's wealth, not least its aggressive neighbour, the Soviet Union. Russian influence pervaded the country and supported Tudeh, the Iranian communist party. Tudeh ordered strikes at various oil installations and the economy of

***After his divorce, the Shah lapsed back into the playboy lifestyle he had enjoyed before his marriage. He became a darling of the gossip columnists, and in little under two years his name was romantically linked with more than 30 women. Newspaper attempts to marry him off became a standing joke at the palace. Among the women whose names were mentioned as possible wives were the glamorous actresses Martine Carol* above, *Sylvia Mangano* near right, *Gene Tierney* mid right, *and Yvonne de Carlo* far right**

John Frost (four pics left)

Iran became destabilized. At the same time, fundamentalist Moslem organizations were openly critical of the Shah.

Assassination attempt

On 4 February 1949, a bitterly cold day when Tehran was blanketed in snow, the Shah had a stark reminder of his own frailty, despite his powerful position. Accompanied by his half-brother, Gholam, he went to the University of Tehran to commemorate its founding. As he stepped out of his Rolls Royce and started up the stairs leading to the Faculty of Law building, a fanatic, bearing the trappings of a news photographer, unleashed a volley of bullets from a Belgian revolver that he had hidden in his fake camera.

Three shots seared harmlessly through the Shah's military cap but the fourth struck his right cheek and came out under his nose. As blood streamed down the Shah's face, his apparently loyal generals, policemen and supporters panicked and dived for cover. Two men remained standing, just a few feet apart. The would-be assassin was pointing a pistol at the Shah's heart.

In an interview 10 years later with his biographer Margaret Laing, the Shah was able to recall every fleeting moment of the incident. 'I had a lucidity that astonishes me even today,' he said. 'I can still remember my reactions at that instant. I thought "What should I do? Jump on him? But if I approach him, I shall become a better target. Shall I run away? Then I shall be a perfect target to be shot in the back." '

Topham

His mind was extraordinarily alert. At the same time as he took note of a cowardly officer who was struggling to crawl under a car, the Shah acted dramatically. He dodged and weaved like a boxer. The gunman fired again but the bullet only creased an Imperial shoulder. Then, in complete silence, click! By chance (the Shah claimed later that it was divine intervention) the revolver had jammed. Seeing a future for themselves, as much as for their Shah, military aides rushed in and clubbed the would-be murderer to death.

Aware that one of his many titles was The Shadow of the Almighty and seeking to show that he was invincible, the Shah wanted to continue his rounds at the university. It was his brother Gholam who persuaded him to go to hospital for treatment.

In 1949, the Shah toured the USA, and was pictured in several night spots. In New York* above *he dined with the daughters of the Brazilian ambassador

***The attempt on his life sobered the 29-year-old Shah and reinforced his sense of destiny. First news reports were that he had been killed, and messages of condolence flooded in from around the world – including from King Farouk, who had continually denounced the Shah since he had renounced Fawzia. The Shah reassured his subjects with a radio broadcast from his hospital bed* below**

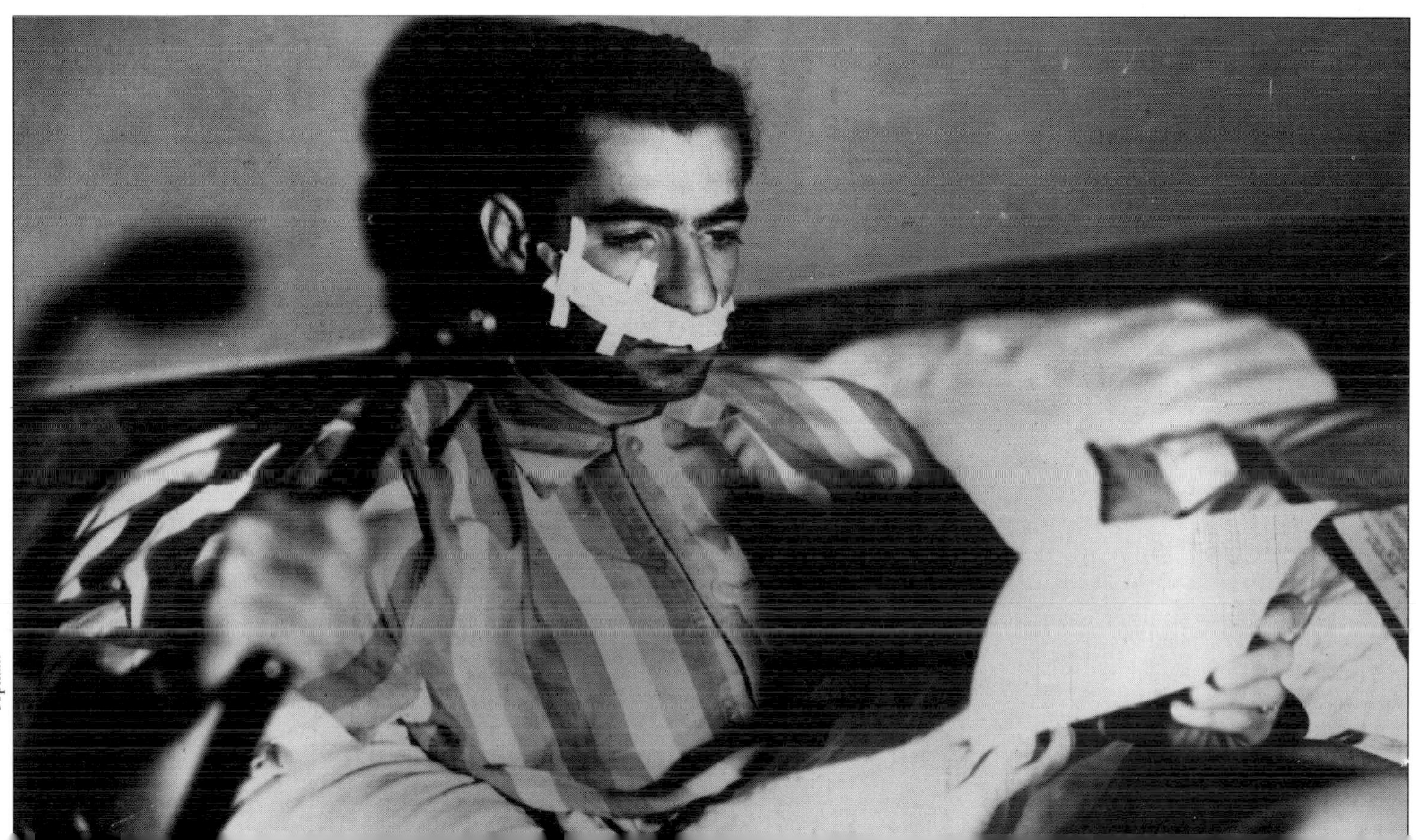

Topham

The five physicians who examined him could find little wrong with the Shah; no bones were broken and the wounds to his face and shoulder were purely superficial. He was back at his palace in the early hours of the morning. But his life would never be the same.

Seizing power

The Shah's close brush with death spurred him into action. The assassin who had tried to kill him was said to be linked both with the Tudeh party and with the conservative religious groups that opposed Iran's links with the West. The King made the most of the prestige attaching to his brave escape, and instituted laws that effectively gave him total power over his country.

Conscious of the fact that he still had no heir to inherit the throne, should another attack on his life be more successful, the Shah decided that it was time to remarry. Ever since his divorce in 1948, Iranian embassies around the world had been on the look-out for a suitable bride for him. Photographs and descriptions of numerous women were presented. But none appealed.

The lovely Soraya

Apparently out of the blue, the Shah learned of a suitable girl in 1950. She was named Soraya Esfandiari. 'I was much impressed by what I heard of her,' he wrote in his memoirs.

The Shah first consulted his old friend, Ernest Perron, the gardener's son from Le Rosey who was now his Personal Secretary. On receiving a positive verdict from his pliable confidant, the Shah felt confident enough to send his elder sister, Princess Shams, on a mission. Her quest was to get a first-hand impression of Soraya.

Soraya happened to be in London at the time and was duly summoned by an innocuous invitation card to attend Shams' royal suite at Claridge's. She was ignorant of any royal intrigue and did not realize that she was to be scrutinized as a potential Empress.

Half Iranian, half German

Highly intelligent and with startling green eyes, Soraya was half Iranian and half German. Her father was an aristocratic and wealthy Bakhtiari chieftain who wielded a considerable amount of power. His home town was Isfahan, and his father had ruled the south-west part of Iran where oil was first discovered. In fact, two of Soraya's uncles had grown so powerful that Reza Khan, the father of the man Soraya was to marry, had ordered that they should be executed.

Soraya's father had been a politics and economics student at Berlin University when he met a Russian-born German girl, Eva Karl. Some 15 months after their first encounter, the couple were married in a Muslim ceremony and for a while they settled in Isfahan. It was here that Soraya was born, on 22 June 1932.

♔ ***The Shah's mother, Tadj-ol-Molouk, was keen to stabilize her son's private life by finding him a wife to bear the son who would preserve the dynasty. She collected photographs of eligible Muslim women from around the world to present to him. The photogenic Soraya Esfandiari*** **below** ***caught the Shah's interest***

Popperfoto

Eva Esfandiari was terrified that her baby might catch one of the many infectious diseases that thrived in the country's unhygienic conditions. Early in 1933 she took the eight-month-old Soraya back to Berlin, but the girl continued to be brought up in the Muslim tradition. When Soraya was five, mother and daughter returned to Isfahan where her father was running a school.

Although Soraya's father was fully versed in Western ways and was indeed adamant that she should have a Western education, he was also determined that his daughter should be aware of her Iranian heritage.

Desert journey

On one occasion, when Soraya was six, father and daughter went for a horse ride across the desert. They left home in the cool of the early morning but by midday the sun was burning hot. Soraya, with a parched throat, asked her father for a drink of water. This was a mistake as, according to tradition, water is supposed to weaken a person's resolve under such condi-

Topham

♔ *Before approaching Soraya, the Shah despatched his sister to London to meet her. First impressions were good, and Soraya* left *accompanied Princess Shams and her husband* far left *on a shopping trip to Paris before flying from Rome to Tehran*

'I was much impressed by what I heard of her'

THE SHAH ON SORAYA

♔ *This formal portrait of the Shah* right *was taken around the time of his engagement to Soraya. After just one meeting, the Shah contacted Soraya's father with a formal proposal. The couple's engagement was announced on 14 October*

Hulton Picture Company

tions. The affronted chieftain angrily spluttered, 'No Bakhtiar woman is ever thirsty,' and they rode on without touching a drop.

Soraya's stay in Iran was brief during her childhood. After a son had been born to Eva, the family escaped the war-torn country and settled near Zurich in 1947. Soraya was first sent to a boarding school in Montreux, but when she was 16 she moved to a finishing school, Les Roseaux in Lausanne.

By the time Soraya was 18, she could already speak fluent German, Persian and French, but her mother insisted that she should learn English as well. She was sent to London and had only been there a short time when she was summoned to Claridge's by Princess Shams.

Soraya learns the secret

After their first successful meeting, Princess Shams invited Soraya to go to Paris with her to do some shopping. By this time, Soraya had an inkling of what Shams' mission was all about. For one thing Soraya's cousin, Gudars Bakhtiari, seemed unduly anxious to take pictures of her. He had been instructed by the Shah to take photographs of his prospective bride, and on Gudars' third visit Soraya wheedled the secret out of him. But, as she said later, 'I did

ST MORITZ: IRAN'S WINTER CAPITAL

The exclusive ski resort of St Moritz *below*, in the Swiss Alps, has long been the winter playground of the jet set. From mid-January to mid-March, the Iranian court – effectively the country's government – operated from Switzerland. Pleasure tended to precede business, and the Shah, his wife and their entourage would spend most of the day on the slopes. Meanwhile, a large administration, operating from two entire floors of the luxurious Grand Hotel Dolder in Zurich, kept in close touch with Tehran and with the Shah's office at the smart Hotel Suvretta in St Moritz.

Alfred Strobel/Camera Press

Topham

Camera Press

♕ ***In the two weeks after their engagement, the Shah and Soraya spent all their free time together, getting to know one another as they explored the countryside around Tehran on horseback or – followed at a discreet distance by armed bodyguards – on foot. Both of them were fond of the outdoor life, and enjoyed several picnics and excursions together as they began to fall in love***

Camera Press

not take any of this seriously.'

In Paris, Princess Shams admitted the truth, saying, 'It would be wonderful if a young woman like you would be willing to share the life of Mohammed Reza.' It was not so much a suggestion, more an order.

A bargain is sealed

In trepidation, Soraya flew to Tehran to meet the Shah. On her first evening in the capital, she was cordially invited to a small family dinner by the Dowager Empress, the Shah's mother. When she arrived at the palace, Princess Shams and the Shah's twin, Princess Ashraf, welcomed her and she was allowed to think that the evening was going to be a soirée with the King's women folk. Just as she was beginning to relax, a manservant opened a door and announced the Shah, clad in his favourite blue Iranian Air Force uniform.

The 19-year-old girl had little time to panic in a situation that had suddenly become very formal. Protocol demanded, for instance, that the Shah's sisters bow to him each time he spoke to them. The Shah, however, did his best to put her at ease. He swung the conversation round to Switzerland, knowing full well that it was a country with which they were both familiar.

The Shah, who had been much taken by the photographs of Soraya – she was very photogenic – was equally captivated by her in the flesh. He noted her expressive eyes, her finely sculpted face and her mane of glossy dark hair. He was also impressed by her poise in what was clearly a demanding situation.

After the lavish dinner, Soraya prepared to make her exit but was halted in her tracks; one of the traditions at the Imperial Court was to play parlour games in the evenings. After a few rounds of charades, during which the tense atmosphere eased, Soraya was able to return to her father's Tehran town-house.

On arriving home, Soraya was faced with endless questions by her father. Finally, he asked, 'Would you be prepared to marry him?' The Shah, it seemed, was not one to waste time and he had already made up his mind; he had sent an emissary round to the house with a formal proposal of marriage and he wanted a reply the very same evening. Soraya, as she wrote later, agreed to marry the Shah 'without a second's hesitation.' Her reply was 'Yes'.

Falling in love

Although Soraya knew that she liked the Shah there was no question of her actually loving him after just one evening together. The same

> **'Don't believe that I can offer you an easy life'**
>
> THE SHAH TO SORAYA

also applied to the King, but his primary aim in marrying was to produce an heir; to him, the need for love was way down the list of wifely qualities. Nevertheless, even he thought it might be wise for them to get to know each other a little before they married, so he arranged for them to meet up as whenever his schedule allowed.

Over the next couple of weeks, the Shah and Soraya were together nearly every day. He drove her up into the mountains outside Tehran in his exotic sports cars and he even took her up in one of his aeroplanes. They also frequently went riding and swimming and Soraya became entranced by her fiancé. 'Had he not inherited the Persian throne he would surely have been a great sportsman and have won Olympic gold medals for Iran,' she said. As for the Shah, he found his bride-to-be charming and delightful; her sense of humour tickled him.

Early on in their courtship, the Shah made it plain to Soraya that political realities meant that their life together would not be a bed of roses. 'Don't believe that I can offer you an easy life. I hope you have no illusions about that,' he told her. She accepted this.

She also came to terms with the doubts that some courtiers and many Iranian people had about her. The fact that she was half European did not make her universally popular. The Shah comforted her by dismissing this criticism. To him, she had the best possible credentials; she was familiar with European habits and ways but remained essentially Iranian in spirit.

Misgivings

Soraya had her own personal misgivings about her decision to marry the Shah; she doubted whether she was good enough for him. Although she came from one of the most respected tribes in Iran, she was not 'royal.' 'I did not come from a Princely family,' she said. She need not have worried on this score because, although Princess Fawzia had come from a long line of Egyptian kings, the Shah himself was born a commoner.

Soraya was also aware that she preferred the sophistication of a European lifestyle to the backwardness of Iran. But, for the time being, she held her tongue and confirmed her commitment to the Shah, whom she was genuinely growing to love.

Poppe-foto

Although she was descended on her father's side from an Iranian tribal chieftain, who had led an insurrection in 1929, her German mother's influence gave Soraya a decidedly independent, Western outlook on life. Though a Muslim, she did not cover her face with the traditional veil, and wore Western clothes. She liked to visit restaurants **above**, ***where she drank wine, forbidden to strict Shi'ite Muslims***

Camera Press

Popperfoto

♔ *In the absence of TV and newspapers, the largely illiterate citizens of Iran learned to recognize their new queen-to-be from banks of photographs on display in the streets and other public places. Official portraits of Soraya* above right *began to appear* above *with those of the Shah and of his daughter by his first marriage, Shahnaz*

THEIR NEW HOME

On one of their excursions together, the Shah drove Soraya to the Ekhtessassi, a comparatively modern house next to the Marble Palace, where the king had lived for a time with his first wife. This, he announced, was to be their home.

Soraya was aghast, for the 12-roomed villa had not been lived in for years and was in a terrible state of disrepair. 'Many of the chairs were damaged, the upholstery and cushions torn, the kitchen quarters in a deplorable state and the servants' rooms mere primitive cells,' she recalled in later years. The Shah, somewhat surprised at Soraya's need for European comfort, conceded that 'a little renovation' might be necessary. In the event the mansion was thoroughly restored.

Close to death

The date for the wedding had been set for 27 December 1950 (the Prophet Mohammed's birthday) but only 18 days after her arrival in Iran, Soraya suddenly fell sick. She had spent the day with the Shah but when she got home in the evening she had a fever. Doctors examined her and diagnosed typhoid. In something of a panic, the Shah ordered physicians to be flown in from abroad but her condition deteriorated and she became very ill indeed.

As she lay close to death, the Shah revealed his love by visiting her bedside every day. He sent her flowers and records and even ordered a film projector to be installed in her room. Just as all hope seemed to be vanishing, a new wonder drug, Aureomycin, was sent from America, and her condition gradually improved.

However, with the wedding just a few weeks away, it became obvious that Soraya would probably be too weak to go through with the ceremony. The date was duly postponed but the Shah grew increasingly agitated – the Muslim period of mourning, lasting two months, started in mid-February and he wanted to get married before then. After a certain amount of cajoling, the doctors agreed that Soraya would be fit enough by early February. The Shah, always a superstitious man, consulted astrologers so that a favourable day could be pinpointed. After studying their charts the astrologers pronounced 12 February a good day.

A relapse

Just as Soraya appeared to be making a good recovery, she had a relapse. Some well intentioned friends had sent her some Swiss chocolate which she could not resist eating. The disease returned to ravage her stomach, and her life was once again in danger.

Soraya's second recovery was slow and the Shah was worried that the wedding would have to be delayed yet again. After consulting her doctors, he reached an acceptable compromise. It was agreed that if most of the formal banquets and balls that were to be a part of the four-day wedding festival were cancelled, then, yes, Soraya would be well enough to go through with a simple ceremony on the prescribed date, 12 February 1951.

Topham

Their serious faces at their betrothal ceremony above ***belied the joy the Shah and Soraya were already beginning to find in each other's company***

A QUESTIONABLE ACE

With his unquenchable love of speed, the Shah took up flying after the war. With only 20 flying hours in his log, he considered himself to be an expert. Events proved otherwise, and one day he damaged his aircraft on landing, ending up with a gash on his forehead. He passed off the cut by explaining that he had accidentally walked into a door.

Unperturbed by his accident, the Shah bought an old Flying Fortress and hired an ex-World War II aviator to teach him how to fly it. Latterly, he did indeed become a good pilot, clocking up more than 5,000 flying hours and investing in several of his own private planes.

AP/Topham

GOLESTAN PALACE

Golestan Palace, or the Palace of Roses, was built at the beginning of the 19th century as a residence for the ruling Qajar kings who in 1788 had moved their seat of government from their ancestral home in Mazandaran to Tehran. Under their rule, the city grew in size and prominence, and later in the century Nasr-ud-din Shah extended the Palace by adding the large first floor hall decorated with mirror work, influenced by interiors he had seen during a European tour in 1873. A modern wing was specially built in this century

All photos William MacQuitty

Set amid pools, fountains and trees, Golestan Palace *left* is a pleasing building characterized by graceful arches, airy windows and a highly decorative façade. The painted tiles, mostly in blue and yellow, which cover much of the exterior depict roses, lions, castles, and pastoral scenes, and dazzle magnificently in the early morning sunlight. The Shah gave Golestan to the nation in 1971 and, although it was used on State and ceremonial occasions, it was also open as a museum

The huge Throne Room *right*, the scene of lavish receptions for foreign dignataries and grand State ceremonies. Displayed in this room were precious gifts given to past Iranian sovereigns, among them a set of Sèvres porcelain, ornamental clocks, cameos, armour, gold plate and magnificent vases of jade. At the end of the room stood the famous Peacock Throne, set with countless precious stones

The honeycombed entrance hall and marble staircase *left* that leads to the sumptuous Throne Room on the first floor of the Palace. Millions of slivers of glass make up the walls and ceiling, creating an impression of overwhelming opulence. Such an excessive display of grandeur in a country dogged by poverty and illiteracy – despite Iran's massive oil reserves – did little to enhance the Shah's diminishing popularity in the later years of his reign

The walls of the Library in Golestan Palace *right* contain panels of etched and embellished mirrors so that the room is imbued with light. Although foreign royalty and high-ranking dignitaries were housed on official visits in the modern wing of the Palace, they had access to magnificent rooms such as this

All photos William MacQuitty

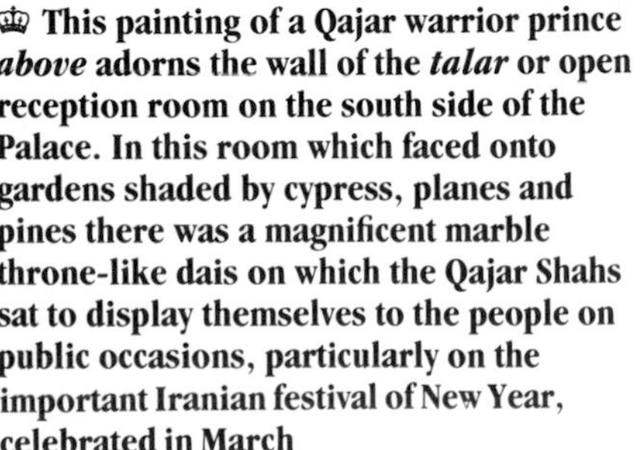

♔ This painting of a Qajar warrior prince *above* adorns the wall of the *talar* or open reception room on the south side of the Palace. In this room which faced onto gardens shaded by cypress, planes and pines there was a magnificent marble throne-like dais on which the Qajar Shahs sat to display themselves to the people on public occasions, particularly on the important Iranian festival of New Year, celebrated in March

♔ A limpid pool graced the area in front of the open reception room *right* during the reign of the Pahlavi dynasty, when people no longer came to pay homage to their ruler in the traditional way. The marble 'throne', however, remained one of the Palace's most impressive treasures, as did the two spiralling stone columns that supported the mirrored ceiling, clearly seen here; both had been brought from Shiraz by one of the Qajar Shahs

♔ The focal point of the Throne Room *above* is the jewel-encrusted Peacock Throne itself, surrounded by a mosaic of mirrors on walls and ceiling. The brilliance of the mirrors is achieved by the use of four small triangular pieces of glass set to form a low pyramid; when these pyramids are repeated endlessly, light is reflected in all directions, creating a spectacular dazzling effect

♔ The intricacy and richness of the Palace's tiled façade *right* is clearly seen here; the lions depicted on either side of the floral, open-worked oval have astrological significance. Mythical beasts support the stone columns of the open portico. Perhaps because it is really a monument to Qajar supremacy, the Golestan Palace was never a favourite with the Shah, who used it almost solely for ceremonial occasions

All photos: William MacQuitty

JOY, DESPAIR, THEN JOY

Robert Harding Picture Library

AS IN A FAIRYTALE ROMANCE, THERE WAS A DAZZLING WEDDING AND THE ROYAL COUPLE HAD A HAPPY START TO MARRIED LIFE. BUT STORMY TIMES LAY AHEAD FOR BOTH OF THEM

AT THE LAST MINUTE, THERE WAS A further change in the wedding arrangements. Tehran in February 1951 was bitterly cold and the Golestan Palace, where the ceremony was to have taken place, was impossible to heat. Now that Soraya was fit enough to go through with the wedding, the Shah banished from his mind the thought of another postponement – it was to be 12 February or never. He decided that the marginally more intimate Marble Palace would not be quite so chilly. Gangs of workmen were ordered to heat the cavernous reception halls and echoing corridors the day before the weddding.

On the day itself, Soraya lived up to her name, which means 'star' in Persian. As the appointed hour approached, she put on her embroidered Dior gown which weighed over 40 pounds. She looked magnificent. The dress was adorned with no less than 6000 diamonds and in her hair she wore a white veil, held in place with a diadem studded with emarelds. The finishing touch was an ermine coat, a gift from Stalin, which she wrapped around her shoulders to keep out the cold.

Well-wishers lining the route from Soraya's home to the palace were few and far

During their whirlwind courtship, the Shah met Soraya nearly every day to go riding* above, *swimming or for drives in his fast sports cars. With each meeting, Soraya's admiration for the Shah grew

The simple wedding ceremony over* below, *the Shah and his slightly nervous 19-year-old bride receive the official congratulations of foreign diplomats in Iran, represented by the Soviet Ambassador

Hulton Picture Company

Soraya* above *arrives at the Marble Palace for her wedding with the Shah's mother and sisters, all swathed in furs against the February chill

Topham

Topham

♔ ***The Shah and his bride*** **above,** ***visibly more at ease, relax after the State dinner held for more than 300 guests at the Golestan Palace on the evening of the wedding. Soraya wears a diadem and emeralds from the Iranian Crown Jewels***

WEDDING PRESENTS

Although their wedding was a comparatively low-key affair, Soraya and the Shah were given presents from many heads of state, particularly those that sought favour with the Shah, who controlled vast oil resources. King George VI gave them a pair of Georgian silver candelabra and President Truman presented them with a huge Steuben glass crystal vase. Stalin gave Soraya the ermine coat that she wore on her wedding day ***left*****.**

To decorate the Marble and Golestan Palaces more than a ton of daffodils, orchids and tulips were specially flown in from Holland and the Iranian Embassy in Rome made a gift of yet more flowers. Ironically, it was the embassy in Rome which refused to acknowledge the Shah two years later when he and Soraya were forced into exile.

Topham

between. Only the extremely hardy and loyal had ventured out into the thick snow. This upset Soraya, as the Shah had decreed that it should be a public holiday and that free food should be distributed to the poor.

Resplendent groom

Any disappointment she might have felt disappeared when she reached the Marble Palace. There, waiting for her at the top of a flight of marble steps, was the Shah, dressed in a dark blue uniform with gold epaulettes and a white sash. She gingerly made her way up the steps towards him, with six girls behind her carrying her long train.

At the top of the flight, the Shah greeted his beautiful bride and led her to the Ivory Room where the wedding ceremony itself was to take place. Following a respectful distance behind came the families of both sides.

On the floor of the Ivory Room, which was lit by gleaming chandeliers, lay a magnificent Persian carpet on which stood two solitary thrones. When the couple were seated, priests set before them the three symbols of a Muslim wedding, the Koran, a mirror and two candlesticks. Then one priest stepped forward and placed the Koran in Soraya's lap.

After reading a short passage from the holy book, the priest asked her two simple questions: did she accept him to be a priest and did she take the Shah to be her husband? She quietly said 'yes' twice. After the priest had put two similar questions to the Shah and he had replied, the couple were pronounced man and wife.

An ordeal

Smiling with happiness, the Shah took his Princess to the Hall of Mirrors to be introduced to their guests. Soraya, however, was not feeling so relaxed. The burden of her weighty dress was taking its toll and she began to feel faint. The Shah ordered maids-in-waiting to remove the heavy petticoats (ten yards of material) that she was wearing under the gown. Soraya, however, still felt ill and had to be helped into a car which promptly whisked her away.

For poor Soraya, the day's events were still not over and in the evening she was obliged to endure a lavish banquet for 300 people in the cold and clammy Golestan Palace. Only then was she free to relax.

A troubled start

Princess Soraya quickly learned that her married life was not going to be easy. For a start, the proposed honeymoon in Switzerland had to be indefinitely postponed because Iran was in political turmoil. That she could accept, but

Topham

♔ ***Both the Shah and Soraya were enthusiastic skiers*** **above** ***and, a few days after their marriage, spent a brief honeymoon enjoying themselves on the slopes near Tehran. After the attempt on the Shah's life, however, he rarely appeared in public without the formidable presence of heavily armed bodyguards, seen here on the right***

what she found more difficult to understand was her husband's domestic lifestyle.

He tended to rise early for work at 7.00 am, while she slept on for a couple more hours. The first time they met during the day was usually for lunch and this was probably the only time when they could chat together freely without interruptions. In the evening, dinner was served at around 7.30, but it was far from being a cosy, intimate meal. 'Almost every evening the entire family was present,' Soraya once said bitterly.

THE DOWAGER EMPRESS

The Shah's mother, Tadj-ol-Molouk, was, in Soraya's words, 'unquestionably the head of the whole dynasty.' Fiery-spirited and courageous, she braved the mullahs' anger in her husband's reign by appearing unveiled; as the foundress of the Pahlavi dynasty, she demanded that her son's wives meet her exacting standards. When they did not, she could make life intolerable as both Fawzia and Soraya learnt to their cost. The Shah rarely questioned her opinions

Hulton Picture Company

When the evening meal was over, the Shah and the Princess, together with his brothers, sisters and meddlesome mother, would retire to play card games or to watch movies in the palace cinema. Even when she had grown accustomed to this routine, Soraya remained irritated by Pahlavi conventions; there appeared to be little genuine warmth between the siblings, who always addressed each other formally.

Perhaps most irksome of all was that there was no sanctuary even in their bedroom. Ernest Perron, the Shah's beloved friend and close adviser, was apt to burst in whenever he wished. 'He was as slippery as an eel,' she once wrote, and she disliked him intensely.

Growing together

It was not the most propitious start to a marriage, but in their fleeting moments of privacy the Shah and Soraya grew to love each other deeply. She was only 19 when she married and he was nearly 12 years older. At first she was star-struck and saw him as a gallant, noble leader, handsome and brave. In many ways he was these things, and as she got to know him better, so her genuine admiration and respect for him grew.

He was extremely self-disciplined and, when it mattered most, courageous. As political strife grew around him, he was forced to make tough decisions and, although he never discussed politics with his wife, she alone

Camera Press

knew how hard it was for him to be decisive. However, she qualified this years later by saying, 'When he had made up his mind he was as hard as steel.'

Both of them were well read and well travelled and they discovered that they had much in common, not least a perverse sense of humour. Soraya had extravagant whims and for some time she kept a pet seal in the fountain of the reception room at the Marble Palace. Nothing amused the Shah more than to watch his wife toss scraps of fish to the animal, which was often allowed to slither across the priceless Persian rugs to fetch its prize.

> ***'When he had made up his mind he was as hard as steel'***
>
> SORAYA ON THE SHAH

Political tension

During their precious moments together, Soraya and the Shah indulged one another and were happy and contented. But political tension was running high in Iran and begun to destroy their tranquility. In public, Soraya rarely appeared to be happy and a vindictive European press dubbed her, 'The Sad Queen Who Never Smiles'.

The Shah had gone to great lengths to try and secure his authority and he was determined that he alone should dictate the fortunes of his country. It was his view that the only way Iran could develop and exploit its huge oil resources was to bring in foreign expertise and aid. The drawback was that the foreign companies took most of the revenue out of the country.

The Shah's main political opponent was Dr Mohammed Mossadeq who succeeded in uniting the Tudeh communist party and ultra-conservative religious fundamentalists in their fight against the monarchy and what was seen as foreign interference. Realizing that Mossadeq had the backing of the people, the Shah reluctantly made the 70-year-old politician Prime Minister in April 1951.

Whiling away the time

By 1953, the Shah had become a puppet king, bereft of genuine power, so he and Soraya spent much of their time in idle pursuits in the confines of the Saadabad Palace, on the outskirts of Tehran. The forceful Princess Ashraf and Tadj-ol Molouk were banished into exile (no doubt to Soraya's glee) and Mossadeq took control of the royal household's expenses. Banquets were forbidden and official functions were kept to a minimum. With little to do during the day, the Shah and Soraya

Popperfoto

♔ ***Happy and contented in these early days of their marriage, the Shah and Soraya* top *relax in the gardens of the Marble Palace with their Alsatian dog and two silk-haired terriers***

♔ ***Soraya* above *takes a brief respite from growing political tension at home by visiting Spain where, as well as more formal duties, she attended a bullfight***

Popperfoto

♛ ***The Shah with Ernest Perron, his Swiss private secretary and closest friend*** right, ***sit alone, dispirited and profoundly depressed, as they wait for the plane to take them to Baghdad and exile***

Fabian Bachrach/Camera Press

♛ ***Wily and ambitious, Dr Mossadeq*** above ***succeeded in ousting the Shah from power and forcing him into exile in 1953. Within days a counter coup was mounted and the Shah returned to a rapturous welcome in Tehran***

passed the time riding, swimming and playing tennis and other games.

In the evening, the Shah, driven by boredom and inactivity, often resorted to playing practical jokes on Soraya and any guests who might be visiting. Soraya once recalled an example of the Shah's humour: 'During the showing of a film there would be a terrific barking of dogs. The startled guests would all turn their heads before they realized that their Emperor in the next room was a superlative dog imitator.'

Soraya herself took up more fulfilling pursuits such as reading. She studied psychology, which she used to good effect in consoling the Shah during his frequent bouts of deep depression. This state of affairs pleased Mossadeq greatly. 'A King should reign not rule,' was one of his favourite sayings.

Muzzling the Shah

Growing increasingly confident, Mossadeq stripped the Shah of much of his personal wealth and disbanded the trusted Imperial Guard. 'I have muzzled the Shah,' announced Mossadeq in mid-1953, but the one powerhouse that he had not won over was the Iranian Army, which stayed loyal to the sovereign.

Fearing that a mob, fuelled by the passion of the Tudeh party, might threaten their lives, the Shah decided that he and Soraya should leave the Saadabad Palace. They moved north and divided their time between a villa on the Caspian Sea and a hunting lodge in the region where Reza Khan had been born. These were comparatively safe places, but the Royal Family was still not out of danger.

Passage to exile

On Sunday 16 August 1953, Mossadeq announced over the radio that the Shah had plotted to overthrow him but that the coup had failed. The Shah now determined that it was time to get out, so he and Soraya flew to Iraq with a few suitcases containing clothes and essential belongings. For two days, the exiled Shah and his wife stayed in the White Palace in Baghdad. The world's press reported that the Pahlavi dynasty was doomed and that, indeed, seemed to be the case.

Thinking that they might be kidnapped or even assassinated in Baghdad, the Shah and Soraya flew to Rome, which they reckoned to be safer. Expecting a welcome from Iran's Ambassador in Rome, the Shah was sorely disappointed. The fickle envoy and many of his staff had thrown in their lot with Mossadeq, thinking that the monarch would never regain his throne.

Angry, sad and exhausted, the exiled couple went to the Excelsior Hotel. Here they learned that the Iranian Foreign Minister had made a radio broadcast denouncing the Shah and demanding that all the Pahlavi family should be executed.

Counter coup

On the morning of 19 August, there was a dramatic turnabout: citizens of Tehran woke up to find the streets filled with tanks and soldiers. The army was staging a counter-coup. The end came for Mossadeq when his house was blown to pieces by a tank. He managed to escape but was arrested later and was subsequently brought to trial for treason.

The return home

Soraya and the Shah were having lunch in their hotel when they heard the news. A journalist rushed into the dining room waving a piece of paper which read, 'Tehran: Mossadeq overthrown. Imperial troops control Tehran.' Fellow diners cheered, Soraya cried and the Shah whispered through tear-filled eyes, 'I knew that they loved me.'

The Shah waited for a few days before returning to Tehran in his own twin-engined plane. At the airport, well-wishers and loyal servants rushed up to him and prostrated themselves at his feet.

As he was driven to the palace from the airport, he noticed that images of himself were once again hanging from public buildings and that his statues were back on their plinths. But there were few people on the streets to welcome him and the roads were lined with infantrymen.

A fortnight after the Shah had been safely installed back in his palace, Soraya joined him. Although the crisis was over, she knew she was flying back to a turbulent future. Years later she hinted that she longed to have a husband who was not burdened and bedevilled by politics. She knew that they would have been much happier together without the constraints of power.

Trusting each other

When they were reunited, Soraya and the Shah were only too aware that their future together looked bleak. Their 12 days in exile had dramatically affected their lives and the only person they could now trust was each other. Their relationship had been strengthened by the period in exile. The Shah had come to value the practical support of his young wife who had shown commonsense and worldly wisdom in the face of trouble. Soraya, in turn, admired her husband's courage and recognized the loneliness and isolation that faced the ruler of a divided country.

Perpetually looking over his shoulder and conscious of the fact that many of his people would like to see him dead, the Shah now acted swiftly on the political front and set up a security network of spies, and spies that spied on spies. Thus was laid the foundations of Savak, the secret security organization which ultimately led to the Shah's final downfall.

AP/Topham

Soraya and the Shah above, *strain showing in the tense expressions on their faces, arrive at Rome airport after fleeing Baghdad and assassination threats. The Shah's efforts to convince his country that Mossadeq's rule would mean Communism and the downfall of the monarchy had temporarily failed*

Topham

The Royal couple, hounded by the Press while walking in the Via Veneto in Rome right, *became virtual prisoners in their luxury hotel while the political crisis lasted. The shattering experience of flight and exile brought the Shah and Soraya closer together but profoundly affected the Shah's political attitudes; security was henceforth rigidly tightened*

'I knew that they loved me'

THE SHAH ON HIS PEOPLE

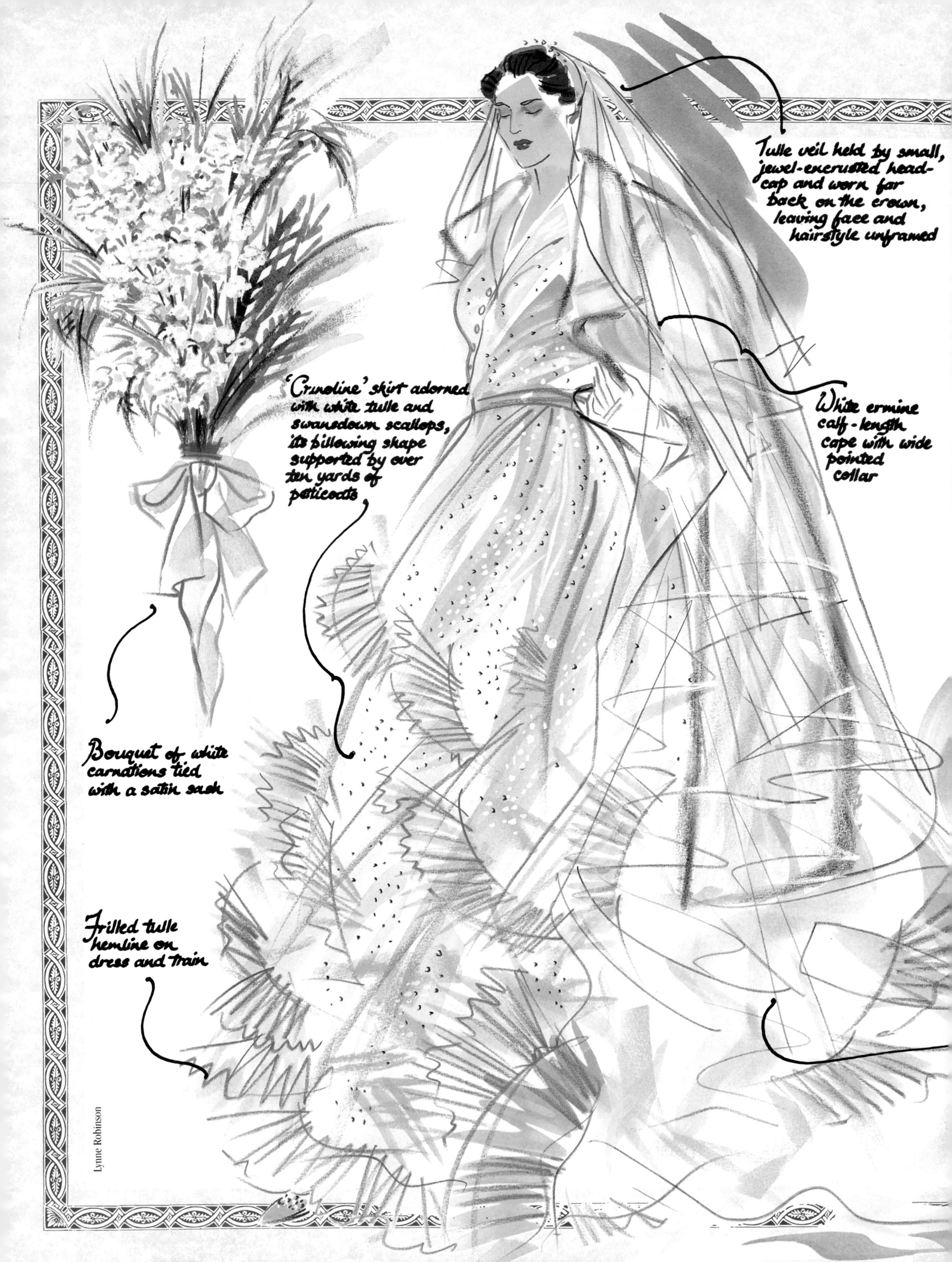
Tulle veil held by small, jewel-encrusted head-cap and worn far back on the crown, leaving face and hairstyle unframed
'Crinoline' skirt adorned with white tulle and swansdown scallops, its billowing shape supported by over ten yards of petticoats
White ermine calf-length cape with wide pointed collar
Bouquet of white carnations tied with a satin sash
Frilled tulle hemline on dress and train
Lynne Robinson

INTERNATIONAL CHIC

One of the most beautiful and glamorous women of her time, Soraya represented the epitome of 1950s chic. Although her frothy, bejewelled ballgowns were designed by top international couturiers such as Dior in Paris and Emilio in Italy, her stylish daywear showed more clearly her own sense of taste, and women all over the world copied her classic tailored suits, jaunty spots and checks and above all her carefully chosen accessories

Fashion designer Emilio of Rome adjusts the folds of a white evening gown especially created by him for Queen Soraya *left*. Made of white organdie, it has a sculpted, strapless bodice embroidered with sequins, which enhances Soraya's slender, youthful figure

Soraya *below* wears a capacious mink coat with a fashionably wide collar as she leaves the Iranian Embassy in London to attend a luncheon at Buckingham Palace given by the Queen and Duke of Edinburgh during a State visit by the Shah and Soraya in 1955

Soraya's splendid wedding dress *left*, a billowing confection of tulle and silver brocade, was designed by Christian Dior. It weighed 40 pounds and its wide skirt was supported by yards of stiff petticoats which, at one stage, had to be cut away by a lady-in-waiting so that the bride could move more easily. So intensely cold was the February wedding day in Tehran that Soraya wore thick woollen stockings under the dress in order to keep warm. The white ermine cape she wore on entering the Palace was a wedding present from Stalin

♔ **Fashionable afternoon wear in the 1950s often featured a full gathered skirt of semi-transparent material such as organza or nylon (at that time a new wonder dress fabric) nipped in and emphasized at the waist by a wide contrasting belt, *left*. Pastel colours were popular as were more vibrant shades such as shocking pink and aquamarine and ming blue**

♔ Soraya, supremely elegant at a polo match in Rome, wears a black and white checked box jacket over a matching frock *left*. The jaunty boater-style hat with its fine veil, and the elbow-length black gloves, complete the sporty look

♔ This portrait photograph of Soraya *below*, taken soon after her marriage, shows her in a simple, classic garment which would not be outmoded today. The satin cuffs are matched by an inset 'bib' in the same material. In general, lack of ostentation characterized Soraya's dress style, as here – except, of course, when State occasions demanded more glittery, showy garments

♔ Pencil-slim skirts topped by well-fitted jackets flaring slightly from the waist *left and below* were a fashionable 'must' in the 1950s but needed expert tailoring and a figure of near-perfect proportions to look good. With her natural grace and poise, and model's figure, Soraya wore this style with stunning effect

Hulton Picture Company

FOR WANT OF AN HEIR

SORAYA AND THE SHAH WERE DEEPLY IN LOVE WITH EACH OTHER BUT A TRAGIC CIRCUMSTANCE FORCED THEM INTO MAKING A DECISION THAT WOULD CHANGE THEIR LIVES FOREVER

♔ ***Princess Soraya captivated foreign visitors with her dignified presence* above *on State occasions, alongside a monarch urgently seeking new authority for his nation. When they travelled abroad, Soraya, seen* below *after arriving in Britain on the* Queen Mary, *touched people with her simple, spontaneous gestures, elegant clothes and gracious, unaffected manners***

Topham

FIRMLY ESTABLISHED BACK ON THE Peacock Throne – at least for the moment – the Shah and Soraya relaxed and began to enjoy themselves. They threw themselves into the social whirl expected of a wealthy, attractive, young royal couple. There were glamorous private film shows, glittering fancy dress balls and lavish parties. The Shah, with Soraya by his side, her hair streaming in the breeze, would race his 120mph Mercedes across the desert, in competition with the fast sports cars of his young rich friends.

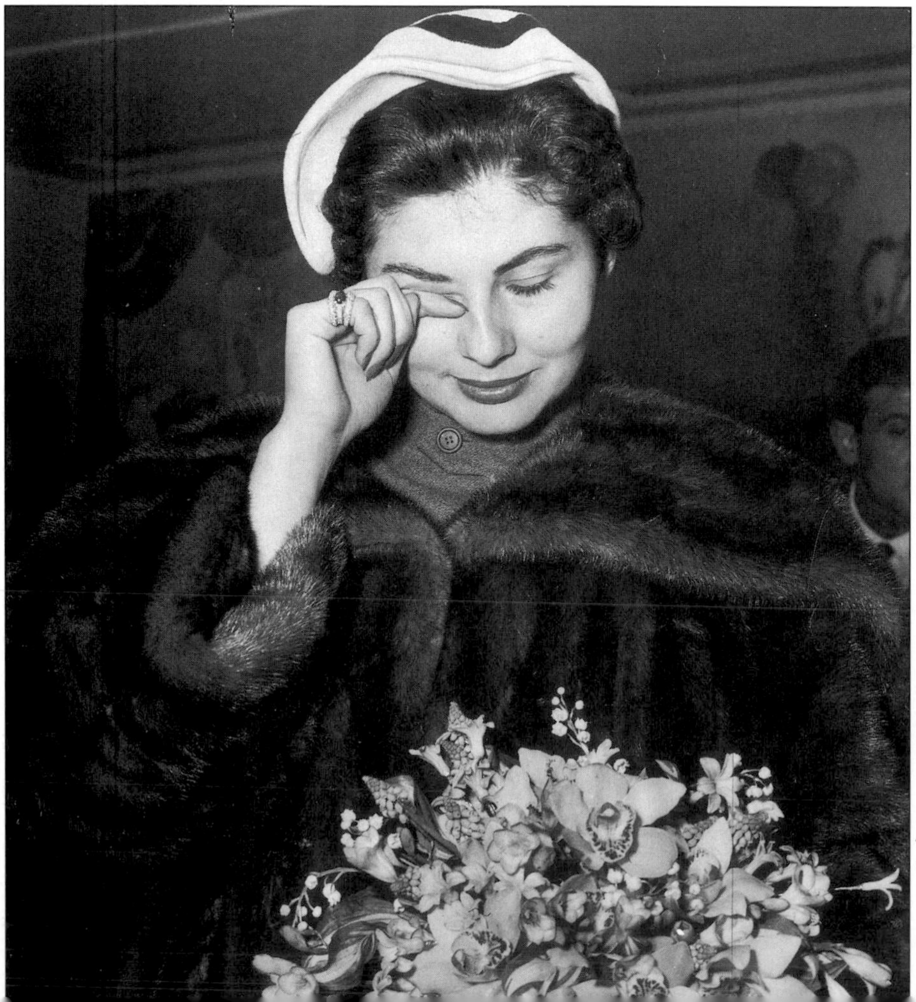

Their public life was also fast-moving. In late 1954 they launched into a series of state visits. Trips to Britain, Germany, Iraq and the USA kept Soraya's picture on the front page of newspapers around the world. Still only 22, she was every inch the glamorous Princess. She soon became the idol of girls everywhere, who copied her fashions and hairstyles. Her hairdresser in Germany set the seal on her fame by selling off locks of her hair.

There was just one problem. After nearly four years of marriage, Soraya showed no signs of becoming pregnant. At first nobody paid much attention to the fact and royal watchers were at least satisfied that the couple were happy together – which was more than could have been said for the Shah's first marriage. However, as time progressed, people began to grow increasingly anxious. 'Who,' they asked, 'is going to inherit the Peacock Throne?'

Smouldering rumours

In Islamic society, producing an heir is considered to be the wife's principal duty, and nowhere was this more acutely felt than in the Pahlavi household. Ugly rumours began to circulate and the guilty party – and guilt is what she surely felt – was assumed to be Soraya, because the Shah had already fathered Princess Shahnaz during his first marriage.

Under the Iranian Constitution, Princess Shahnaz, being a woman, was not eligible to inherit the throne. The Shah's younger brother, Ali, was next in line but he hardly had the stomach to rule. 'His only passion was hunting,' Soraya said of him. The Shah's half-brothers were also ineligible because of Qajar blood on their mother's side (the long-established Qajar dynasty ruled Iran before Reza Khan usurped the throne).

The pressure on the Shah and Soraya became intense and, although he protected

Army officers wearing black arm bands carried the body **right** *of Prince Ali Reza, the Shah's brother, from Tehran's Sepah Salar Mosque to the Shahr Rey Mausoleum on 4 November 1954. The Prince* **inset** *had little influence on Iranian politics but his sudden death changed the course of the Pahlavi dynasty. From then on, an anxious Shah allowed the need for a son and heir to shatter his tranquillity, spawn Palace feuds and destroy his marriage*

Topham

Camera Press

his wife from the ceaseless gossip, she was not immune to the controversy surrounding her. She was made to feel that she was letting down the entire nation.

On 26 October 1954, Prince Ali was at the cotton plantation he owned on the shores of the Caspian Sea. In the afternoon, he summoned his pilot and asked to be flown back to Tehran so that he could attend the Shah's 35th birthday party. The pilot had his doubts about the wisdom of the flight because storms had been forecast. The Prince, realizing that the journey over the Elburz Mountains in a three-seater plane might be foolhardy, was about to cancel the flight when some peasants ran on to the airfield bearing a sick man on a stretcher. The man was dying of pneumonia and the peasants begged the Prince to fly him to a Tehran hospital which might be able to save his life. Ali succumbed to their pleas and, at six o'clock, the light aircraft took off.

> **'All Persians used to sit, eat and sleep on the floor. It is not possible to change this overnight'**
>
> SORAYA ON THE SHAH'S TASK

Back in Tehran, during the evening's festivities, the Shah and Soraya grew increasingly anxious that Ali had not arrived. Anxiety turned to despair. A week later search parties found the wreckage of the plane with three bodies in it.

Ali's death shocked both the Shah and the country. 'I have never known the Shah so sad,' Soraya said. 'He reproached himself for never having let his brother see how much he loved him.' The Shah was also deeply concerned because there was now nobody who could take over should anything happen to him.

Pressure mounts

Soraya could find little peace, even within the confines of the palace walls, after Ali's death. Ernest Perron, the Shah's Private Secretary, relentlessly quizzed her. Day after day, he plied her with personal questions about her marriage, and ultimately made her feel, as a barren woman, a disgrace to Iran. In private conversations with the Shah, Perron urged him to produce an heir – or get rid of Soraya.

Her patience exhausted, Soraya pleaded

Iran's Royal couple **below** *manage an air of serenity on arrival in New York in December 1954. Few people knew the anxieties behind the façade. Both were to enter hospital for tests which would, they hoped, establish whether they could have children*

Popperfoto

Hulton Picture Company

The Shah had once warned Soraya that their life as man and wife would never be easy. She was too young to understand fully what he meant until she was hopelessly entangled in the intrigues of both the Court and the family. Dismay, sorrow and disappointment show on her face in this formal study above. *Although she continued to appear by his side, she had come to feel a failure to her husband and the country he ruled*

with her husband to dismiss Perron, but he would have none of it. He saw Perron as his only ally and friend among the treacherous sycophants who tried to gain favour at the royal palace.

The Shah's family gave Soraya little support either. Indeed, they positively rubbed salt into her wounded pride. Tadj-ol-Molouk, her mother-in-law who was now back from exile, let it be known that she thought Soraya useless as a woman. Similarly, the Shah's sisters failed to rally round.

The only person who remained loyal to her was the Shah. Although he had refused to banish Ernest Perron, he strenuously tried to protect her from the increasing hostility that pervaded not just the palace, but the streets of Tehran as well.

A month after Ali's funeral, Soraya and the Shah flew to New York and were admitted to the Presbyterian Medical Centre in Manhattan, where they were both examined by specialists. 'We can find no reason why Your Majesty should not become a mother,' announced the doctor who saw Soraya. 'You must be patient.' When the Princess asked if there was anything that could be done to hasten her chances of becoming pregnant, she was told, 'No, it is pointless, it's simply a question of time.'

New horizons

This news greatly cheered the Shah and Soraya and, temporarily relieved of pressure, they took a brief honeymoon by extending their stay in America before returning to Tehran.

Back home, the couple, happy and reassured, were optimistic. Fired with a new fervour, the Shah unveiled an ambitious plan aimed at developing his country. But in Iran certain customs were immemorial and such plans take time to get under way and cynics soon claimed that the idea was just a way of currying favour with the masses.

> ***'Increasingly I realized that the high interests of the nation required an heir'***
>
> THE SHAH

At the same time, Soraya, still only in her early twenties, took heart from her husband's example and ventured into taking on some modest social work. However, somewhat arrogantly, she took time off now and again to visit Tehran's Central Bank to demand access to the Imperial Crown Jewels. She was affronted when the bank demanded receipts for the jewels she wished to requisition and was especially upset when they demanded a date of return.

Over an 18-month period, Soraya undoubtedly became more confident and relaxed. But she still did not become pregnant.

If the Shah was unfailingly gentle and kind to Soraya in the months that followed their American trip, the same could not be said of his dealings with many of his subjects. He

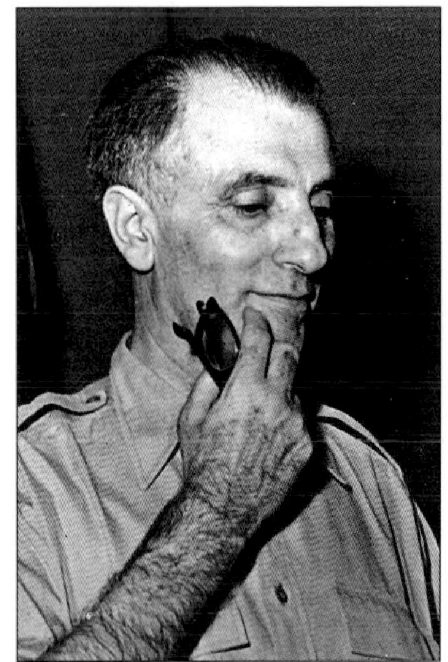

Camera Press

In the game of Iranian power, the fortunes of General Fazlollah Zahedi **above** *rose and fell. The Shah's military backer and Prime Minister, he was ordered to resign when his efforts to dislodge the Shah became too obvious. He did so with grace and safety*

Popperfoto

Iran suffered from appalling illiteracy. The Shah committed public funds to dragging the country into a thriving, modern era with improved skills and education. He and the Princess **above** *dressed informally on their many visits to classrooms*

became increasingly paranoid about his vulnerability. Not only did he have no heir but his schedule often took him out of Tehran. He thought, probably rightly, that anybody with enough clout could oust him from the throne while he was away from his power base.

He was devoted to his country and he desperately wanted it to progress and succeed. But he also wanted any such developments to be firmly under his control. He was suspicious of just about everybody and his network of spies continually relayed information to him on who was gaining authority. Soraya, in her wisdom, preferred to ignore Iran's politics but, on occasion, even she was stunned by the Shah's ruthlessness. In a country suffering upheavals such as Iran was no surprise that the Shah should order Communist leaders to be executed, but he also regularly dismissed Prime Ministers to undermine their own ambitions for replacing his rule.

Resignation

The Shah, however, lacked the thoroughgoing ruthlessness of his father. On one notable occasion, a Prime Minister, General Zahedi, was ushered into the palace while the Shah and Soraya were taking tea in the warmth of the afternoon. To Soraya's astonishment, Zahedi announced his resignation, pleading illness as the reason.

General Zahedi was the man who had lead the counter-coup in 1953 that brought the Shah back from exile. Overwhelmingly grateful at the time, the Shah made him Prime Minister. However, a year later spies revealed that Zahedi was becoming increasingly ambitious and the Shah supposed that his erstwhile saviour might soon attempt to take control of

THE PEACOCK THRONE

The Iranian monarchy was known as 'The Peacock Throne'. The original, actual Peacock Throne was looted by Nadir Shah in the early 19th century when he captured the Red Fort in Delhi. Nadir was so taken by the bejewelled chair that he ordered a divan of similar design, specifying that it should be festooned with gems. Nadir returned to Persia with both 'thrones' but lost them in a war with the Kurds, who distributed the diamonds, emeralds, rubies and pearls among their favoured generals.

A Qajar shah subsequently ordered a copy of the original Nadir armchair to be made and it was on this replica that the Shah (in 1967) and his father crowned themselves. This replica throne was dazzling – it contained an astonishing 26,733 precious gems. It was subsequently destroyed.

Camera Press

Popperfoto

♔ *The strains of a disintegrating relationship are all too obvious on the Royal couple* above *in 1957. Both realized that, despite their love for each other, divorce was almost inevitable. Ironically, the reason for the divorce was to ensure the survival of the Pahlavi dynasty*

♔ *After her divorce, which she had no power to contest, a distraught Soraya turned to her family in Germany for solace. With her mother* below *she arrived in Genoa, Italy, to sail for a holiday in America*

Popperfoto

the country. The Shah had made it plain to Zahedi that he should go.

The Shah's father would most likely have ordered the outgoing premier to be executed but Mohammad Reza was more generous and perhaps wiser. Instead of the gallows, he offered Zahedi an ambassadorship, which was gratefully accepted.

Fate in the balance

By the end of 1957, the Shah's relationship with Soraya was under strain. There was no doubt that he loved her dearly but there was also a lot at stake if she did not give birth to a son. 'Increasingly I realized that the high interests of the nation required an heir,' he jotted in his memoirs. The impact of the inevitable had not escaped Soraya either and she became more and more depressed.

Had the Shah not been absolute ruler of a nation which demanded that his wife bear a son, she would surely have found contentment in their genuinely loving marriage. As it

> ***'I am still deeply in love with Soraya. I destroyed my personal life for my country'***
>
> THE SHAH

was, Islamic tradition and the Iranian Constitution wore down the resolve of her otherwise valiant husband. Though he had adopted many Western ways, staying loyal to his lover became an impossibility.

Soraya, despite her years in Europe and the fact that she was half German, accepted that her fate would not be ruled by love but rather by tradition. She was, after all, familiar with Persian ways and she acknowledged that the man she loved so much must ultimately have an heir. Otherwise, the Pahlavi dynasty would be lost forever.

In a desperate attempt to keep their marriage together, Soraya suggested to the Shah that the law which prevented descendants of the Qajar family from inheriting the throne might be changed. If this ban were lifted, one of the Shah's Qajar half-brothers could be declared heir to the throne.

At first, the Shah refused to accept the idea. The alternative, however, as Soraya frankly told him, was divorce. The Shah could not bear to part from Soraya and, though he

ISLAMIC DIVORCE

Under Islamic law, as prescribed by the Koran, a man can divorce a wife (he can, theoretically, have several) for many reasons. Adultery, incompatibility and cruelty are among them. However, some marriage contracts include the clause that should a wife prove barren, that can be grounds for divorce. It was under such a contract that the Shah managed to estrange himself from Soraya.

Although Islamic teaching may seem unfairly harsh on women, it does, however, prescribe rights to wives that would not be acceptable in Christian-based law. For example, and to quote the Shah's own words, 'a woman could complain if the man did not visit her bed after three months.'

had given up hope that his wife would have a son, he agreed to put the plan to the Council of Elders.

He summoned the Council early in 1958. On 13 February, Soraya tactfully left Iran while her future was under consideration. With a heavy heart, she flew to the ski slopes of St Moritz, where the Shah owned a villa.

An anxious wait

As the days passed, Soraya waited nervously for news of the Council's deliberations. She telephoned her husband on several occasions and he sounded forlorn as hope faded.

After a month, three emissaries arrived in Switzerland. The Council had refused to lift the ban. There was, however, a chance of saving the marriage. If Soraya would agree to the Shah taking a second wife, as was his right under Islamic law, then Soraya and the Shah could remain together. She refused.

Deep sorrow

It came as no surprise to the hapless Princess when a rudely quick divorce was announced on 14 March. The Shah, choked with emotion, made a broadcast to the nation. He confessed to having a 'deep sorrow' before he was cut off the air. A humiliated and distressed Soraya also conceded that the marriage was over. A terse account of Soraya's feelings was reported in *The Times*. It said that she was intent on 'disregarding her personal feelings and the bonds of affection uniting them, to preserve the high interests of the state'.

Soraya immediately flew to Munich in Germany to be with her parents. She was given a handsome allowance, but an uncertain and lonely future lay ahead. As for the Shah, a new hunt began to find him a young bride who would produce the essential heir. Desolate and grief-stricken, the Shah remained incommunicado for several months. 'I am still deeply in love with Soraya,' he said. 'I destroyed my personal life for my country.'

All memory of Soraya's existence in Tehran was officially removed.

Topham

Grim and distracted, the Shah welcomes guests* above *inside the Royal Palace, less than two weeks after Soraya was effectively banished. Without her queenly presence and charm, the Shah looked a hapless man, unable to provide the touch of personal mystique a monarch requires to win support

Topham

The solitary figure of the Shah* left, *deprived by political necessity of the woman he loved, walks alone in the gardens of the Royal Palace in the first days after they were divorced. The couple had said no proper farewell to each other in the tense atmosphere as Iran's fate for a generation was created

A Sporting Life

The Shah's interest in sports began when he was a schoolboy in Switzerland and remained one of his lifelong passions. He was a born athlete who, when young, excelled at football and tennis and later at skiing. During their marriage, the Shah and Soraya spent some of their happiest moments together riding, swimming, sailing, skiing and even watching sports both at home and abroad

Topham

The Shah and Soraya *above* enjoy a soft drink as they watch the Davis Cup tennis match in Paris in June 1957. The Shah himself was a fine tennis player and a keen follower of international tennis events

Popperfoto

During a State visit to India in 1956, the Shah and Soraya *right* take time off to participate in an elephant hunt in the Mysore forests. This 'rogue' elephant was shot by the Shah personally